CODEUS

(Co-De-Us)

The Future Of Barcodes

How blockchain tokenization will transform how the world uses the common barcode.

Erik Quisling

Cover Design & Layout by Erik Quisling

Library of Congress Cataloging-in-publication Data

07 06 05 04 03   5 4 3 2 1
First Edition

Quisling, Erik
      CODEUS: The Future of Barcodes. How blockchain tokenization will transform how the world uses the common barcode. / Erik Quisling;

Edited by Erik Quisling
      p. cm.

ISBN-13: 978-1-936965-63-2

Library of Congress

1. Technology 2. Futurist 3. Barcodes 4. Entertainment 5. Quisling, Erik

Upaya House Publishing
8173 Auberge Circle
San Diego, CA 92127

Printed in USA

CODEUS

(Co-De-Us)

The Future
Of Barcodes

Table of Contents

Part III: CODEUS Applications

What is a CODEUS Global Code?
Creating a Global Code
Applications Across Industries
Consumer Products
Electronics
Fashion & Luxury Goods
Food & Beverage
Pharmaceuticals

Part IV: CODEUS AccelPass

Vision: A Night to Remember
Arrival: A Wallet That Greets You
Entry: Tap & Go
Inside: Gamified, Personalized, Alive
Interactions: Queue-Free Everything
The Show: You're Part of It
After the Show: The Night Lives On
Sporting Events Application
Business Model Innovation

What is CODEUS SecurePass?
Vision: Trust at Every Scan
At the Store: Scan for Truth
After Purchase: Ownership Transfer
Going Deeper: The Origin Trail
Resale or Recycling: A New Life
Supply Chain Manager Perspective
Manufacturing: The Origin Point
Packaging & QA: Verified Before Movement
Shipping: Blockchain Meets Logistics
Warehousing: Real-Time Inventory Intelligence
Retail Distribution: Traceable to the Shelf
Returns, Recalls, or Recycling: Instant Resolution
The Problem It Solves
Key Features

Part V: The Transformation

Introduction

A Vision of 2030

The alarm on Maya's phone chimes softly. She reaches for the nightstand, but not for her phone—for the amber bottle of vitamins she takes each morning.

She taps the bottle's barcode with her phone. Instantly, a verification screen appears: **Authenticated. Manufactured March 2030. Cold chain maintained. No recalls. Purity: 99.8%.**

Five years ago, she wouldn't have trusted the supplement industry. Counterfeit vitamins had flooded the market, indistinguishable from legitimate products until people got sick. Now, every bottle tells its complete story—from the farm where the ingredients were grown to the facility where they were processed, all verifiable on the blockchain.

She swipes to see the origin: organic ashwagandha from a certified farm in India, harvested sixty-three days ago.

She takes the vitamin and heads to her closet.

Marcus pulls into the stadium parking lot three hours before kickoff. His phone vibrates as he crosses the lot entrance—his season pass has already authenticated his arrival and assigned him VIP parking in section A2. No ticket to show. No QR code to fumble with. The blockchain knows who he is, what he owns, and what he's entitled to.

As he walks toward the gate, his AccelPass wallet updates: **Welcome back, Marcus. Superfan Level: Gold. 847 lifetime engagement points. You're in the top 2% of season ticket holders.**

He smiles. Those points weren't just for showing up—they were earned. Every merchandise purchase, every concession stand visit, every halftime trivia challenge he participated in last season accumulated into a verified digital record that traveled with him. The team recognized loyalty now, not just attendance.

At the gate, he taps his phone against the reader. The screen flashes green: **Section 112, Row 5, Seat 14. Fast-Pass Active. Pre-ordered nachos ready at Gate C.**

Inside, the stadium feels alive in a way it never did before. Every screen around the concourse displays real-time fan engagement leaderboards. Sponsors offer instant rewards for scanning branded codes throughout the venue.

Marcus scans a Gatorade display and unlocks 10 bonus points plus a limited-edition NFT featuring his team's star quarterback.

By the fourth quarter, he's earned enough points to unlock exclusive post-game content: locker room interviews, behind-the-scenes footage, and an AR experience that lets him relive the winning touchdown from the quarterback's perspective.

When he gets home that night, his AccelPass wallet contains more than memories—it holds verified proof of attendance, three digital collectibles, and an invitation to an exclusive season ticket holder event next month.

His friend texts him asking if he's willing to sell his collectible NFT of the game-winning play. Marcus checks the marketplace. It's already worth three times what he'd expected.

He decides to hold onto it.

Across town, Sarah stands in a luxury boutique examining a handbag. It's beautiful—buttery leather, impeccable stitching, and a price tag that makes her pause. But she's been burned before. Last year, she bought what she thought was an authentic designer bag online, only to discover months later it was a sophisticated fake.

Not this time.

She pulls out her phone and scans the barcode inside the bag's interior pocket. The CODEUS SecurePass interface loads immediately:

Authentic. Manufactured in Florence, Italy. Artisan ID: G.Rossi. Production date: February 12, 2030. Material: Full-grain Tuscan leather, certified sustainable source. Journey: Florence → Paris Distribution Center → New York Import → Your City.

She taps "View Full Journey" and a timeline appears showing every checkpoint—photos of the workshop where it was made, the artisan who crafted it, customs documentation, and even the carbon footprint of its journey to this boutique. Every step is cryptographically verified and immutably recorded.

But here's what seals the deal: she taps "Resale Value" and sees that this particular bag, because of its verified authenticity and documented provenance, has actually appreciated in value on the secondary market. If she ever wants to sell it, she can transfer the blockchain ownership token to the buyer instantly, and they'll have the same confidence she has now.

She buys the bag.

Three years later, when she decides to sell it, the transaction takes ninety seconds. The new owner scans the code, verifies the complete history including Sarah's ownership period, and transfers payment. Sarah receives 95% of the sale price; the brand automatically receives a 5% royalty encoded into the smart contract when the bag was first tokenized.

Everyone wins. No counterfeits. No disputes. No uncertainty.

In a warehouse outside Chicago, David oversees the receiving dock for a major electronics retailer. A shipment of smartphones arrives from overseas—2,000 units that will be distributed to stores across the Midwest.

Ten years ago, this process took hours of manual checking, paperwork, and database entries. Counterfeit devices regularly slipped through. Gray market products ended up where they shouldn't. Recalls were nightmares of incomplete records and liability exposure.

Now, David watches as his team scans the master container code. Instantly, the blockchain verifies every phone inside:

Container #ZH-4471-B. Contents: 2,000 units. Model: Apex Pro 15. Serial numbers: Verified. Origin: Shenzhen facility #3. Quality control: Passed. Compliance: US/EU standards met. Chain of custody: Unbroken.

The system flags one anomaly: three units show a temperature excursion during shipping—they spent forty minutes outside the recommended thermal range during a customs delay. David quarantines those units for additional testing. In the old system, they would have gone straight to store shelves. Someone would have bought a potentially defective phone, and the company would have dealt with the warranty claim months later.

Not anymore.

The remaining 1,997 phones are automatically added to inventory, their blockchain records synced with the retailer's system. When customers buy these phones in stores next week, they'll be able to scan the barcode and see the entire verified journey—from the factory floor to their hands.

And when those customers eventually sell or trade in their phones, the next owner will have the same transparency. The phone's complete history—every owner, every repair, every accessory purchase—travels with the device permanently.

David remembers the chaos of the old system, the counterfeit scandals, the recall disasters. He doesn't miss any of it.

At a pharmaceutical distribution center, an alert sounds on Dr. Patel's dashboard. A batch of insulin has been flagged. Not because it's counterfeit—the blockchain verification is clear. Not because it's expired—the cold chain monitoring shows perfect temperature compliance throughout its journey from manufacturer to distributor.

It's flagged because the FDA has just issued a voluntary recall for a specific lot number due to a packaging defect discovered at another facility.

In the old system, this recall would take days to execute. Companies would issue press releases. Distributors would check warehouses manually. Pharmacies would search their shelves. Some affected products would inevitably reach patients. Some wouldn't be found for weeks.

With CODEUS SecurePass, Dr. Patel's system identified every unit from the affected lot in 3.2 seconds. The blockchain knows exactly where every vial is—which warehouses, which pharmacies, which patients have already received prescriptions. Automated notifications go out instantly. Pharmacies are alerted. Patients who received the affected lot get direct messages with instructions.

Within two hours, 99.7% of the affected product is located and quarantined. No one is harmed. The manufacturer's liability is limited. The recall costs a fraction of what it would have in the past.

More importantly, every vial of insulin in the system is verifiable. Counterfeit medications— which once killed thousands annually—have virtually disappeared from legitimate supply chains.

When a patient picks up their prescription, they can scan the barcode and know with absolute certainty that what they're holding is authentic, properly stored, and safe.

The technology that makes this possible isn't revolutionary sci-fi. It's a barcode—the same type of barcode that's been on products for fifty

---

years. But now, that barcode is a key to the blockchain, unlocking a dimension of trust, transparency, and traceability that was impossible before.

The Morning After Tomorrow

These aren't fantasies. They're glimpses of a world already being built—a world where every product tells its story, every ticket is a smart asset, every transaction is verifiable, and every barcode is more than just a number.

This is the world CODEUS makes possible.

The technology exists. The infrastructure is being deployed. The question is not whether this future will arrive, but how quickly it will become the standard we all expect.

Welcome to CODEUS.

Welcome to the future of barcodes.

Part I:

Understanding the Foundation

Chapter 1:

What is a UPC Barcode?

To understand where we're going, we must first understand where we are.

A UPC barcode is fundamentally a unique, 12-digit number that nobody else in the world has. The black lines are simply a specialized font (UPC-A) that correlates exactly to the numbers beneath them. Computer scanners read these vertical lines more easily than curved numbers, especially older scanning technology.

Think of a UPC as a social security number for each product. That's all it is—a unique identifier.

The critical aspect: **all UPC barcode numbers must originate from the same database** to ensure global uniqueness. Since the early 1970s, that database has been managed by GS1, a private consortium owned by major retailers including Walmart, Kroger, Home Depot, and Lowe's.

How UPC Barcodes Work

Barcodes serve as convenience tools for retail stores. When you sell a product at a retailer, they have you complete a product information form containing your company details, product specifications, price, and your 12-digit UPC number. The retailer manually enters this information into their inventory management system. When they scan your barcode at the register, it retrieves that product information.

You receive credit for the sale, and inventory decreases by one unit.

Your barcode is the link between your physical product and its digital record in the retailer's system.

The Global Standard

UPC barcodes work anywhere in the world. While some countries use 13-digit EAN (European Article Number) barcodes, a 12-digit UPC functions universally. EAN scanners automatically add a leading zero to convert UPC codes, but UPC scanners in North America cannot read EAN codes. Therefore, a UPC provides global compatibility, while an EAN limits you geographically.

This universality makes UPC the de facto standard—but also reveals its limitations. The barcode itself contains no information beyond that unique number. Everything else—product details, ownership, authenticity, history—lives in separate, centralized databases that are siloed, vulnerable, and limited.

Chapter 2:

What is a QR Code?

QR codes represent a more recent evolution in barcode technology, though they serve a fundamentally different purpose.

A QR code is simply a web address encrypted into a two-dimensional matrix format. When you scan a QR code with your phone's camera, it launches that web address in your browser. The code doesn't contain the actual content—just the URL pointing to it.

Originally invented in Japan in 1994 for automotive parts tracking, QR codes have become ubiquitous for menu access, payment systems, and marketing campaigns. However, like UPC barcodes, they remain passive pointers to external information rather than autonomous containers of verifiable data.

QR codes hint at what's possible—embedding more information in a scannable format—but they still depend entirely on centralized servers and lack any mechanism for verification, ownership, or permanence.

Part II:

The Blockchain Foundation

Chapter 3:

Understanding Blockchain Technology

In the modern digital age, trust is typically mediated by third parties—banks, governments, or corporations. These entities manage records, authorize transactions, and verify identities. Blockchain technology offers a powerful alternative: a decentralized, transparent, and secure method to record and verify information without relying on central authority.

Core Principles

At its foundation, a blockchain is a distributed database that organizes information into blocks. These blocks contain data—often transactions—and are chronologically linked to form a continuous chain. Once a block is completed and added to the chain, it becomes immutable and transparent.

Every block contains a cryptographic reference to the previous block, creating a secure link throughout the entire chain. This structure makes retroactive alteration incredibly difficult; changing a single block would require altering every subsequent block across every copy of the blockchain in existence.

Decentralization as Security

Rather than being stored in a single location or managed by one entity, the blockchain exists simultaneously across a network of computers called nodes. Each node maintains a complete copy of the entire blockchain and works collaboratively to verify new transactions. This decentralization increases security and resilience—there is no single point of failure and no centralized control vulnerable to corruption or manipulation.

Transparency and Immutability

Blockchain is fundamentally transparent. In most public blockchain networks, all transactions are visible to anyone. This openness creates accountability where actions can be traced and verified without compromising privacy. Advanced cryptographic methods ensure that once information is recorded, it cannot be altered retroactively without network consensus.

Smart Contracts

Beyond simple record-keeping, blockchain supports "smart contracts"—self-executing agreements with terms written directly into code. These contracts automatically enforce themselves when predefined conditions are met, eliminating intermediaries and reducing potential for fraud or dispute.

Applications Beyond Currency

Supply chain management can provide transparent tracking of goods from origin to shelf, ensuring authenticity and ethical sourcing. Identity verification can offer secure, user-owned digital identities that reduce fraud. Voting systems can ensure tamper-proof elections with verifiable audit trails. Event ticketing systems can transform tickets into digital assets with embedded rights and ownership.

Blockchain represents a paradigm shift in how we manage data, verify trust, and build systems of record. By eliminating the need for central authorities and introducing transparent, decentralized ledgers, blockchain opens possibilities for fairness, accountability, and innovation in the digital world.

Chapter 4:

Blockchain Tokenization

In the digital transformation of supply chains, entertainment, and commerce, blockchain tokenization stands as a critical enabler. Within the CODEUS ecosystem, tokenization is not merely a technical feature—it's the foundation for how barcodes become smart, verifiable digital assets that unlock new forms of trust, engagement, and monetization.

What is Tokenization?

Tokenization is the process of converting a physical or digital asset into a cryptographically secure digital token that exists on a blockchain. These tokens represent rights to an asset— such as ownership, access, or authenticity—and can be programmed, transferred, or audited through smart contracts.

Unlike traditional data systems where barcodes are static identifiers linked to external databases, CODEUS reimagines the barcode as a living tokenized asset. Each CODEUS barcode becomes a blockchain-registered token with built-in metadata, ownership history, usage rules, and expiration logic—all stored immutably on-chain.

Why Tokenize Barcodes?

Traditional barcodes are passive; they encode only an identifier. Their functionality is limited to pointing to an external source of truth, such as a SKU or URL.

Tokenized barcodes offer a new paradigm:

- **Proof of Authenticity**: The token verifies whether the barcode is valid and issued by the rightful authority

- **Transferable Ownership**: Barcodes can be transferred like NFTs, enabling resale, gifting, or delegation

- **Integrated Logic**: Tokenized barcodes can expire, activate based on conditions, or trigger automated actions

- **On-Chain Metadata**: Brand, model, issue date, and associated value live directly within the barcode token—no external database required

CODEUS Implementation

In CODEUS, each barcode is minted as a unique digital token stored on a public blockchain. The system supports both fungible tokens (for commodity SKUs) and non-fungible tokens (NFTs, for serialized or event-specific assets like tickets or luxury goods).

When a user scans a barcode, they aren't just accessing data—they're querying the blockchain in real time to verify its state and history.

Each CODEUS barcode token includes:

- A unique barcode hash or encoded image

- Metadata (product info, issuer, value, expiry)

- Smart contract logic (redeemability, revocation rules)

- Ownership and transfer history

- Links to media assets via IPFS or Arweave (visuals, documents, warranties)

This structure allows CODEUS to support applications ranging from verifying limited edition products to transferring concert ticket ownership to enabling blockchain-powered warranties for electronics.

Comparison: Traditional vs. Tokenized

Feature	Traditional Barcode	CODEUS Tokenized Barcode
Ownership tracking	✕	☑
Programmability	✕	☑ (smart contracts)
Transferability	✕	☑
Tamper-proof verification	✕	☑ (on-chain proof)
Integrated metadata	✕	☑
Secondary market support	✕	☑
Event-based usage	✕	☑

Real-World Impact

For consumers, tokenized barcodes enable portable ownership, access to authentic goods, and assurance against counterfeits.

For brands, it creates a direct channel for post-sale engagement, resale royalties, loyalty rewards, and deeper insight into how products move through the world.

For developers and marketplaces, tokenized barcodes become programmable building blocks—enabling smart contracts for refunds, resale limits, warranty activation, and real-time analytics.

A New Asset Class

In the CODEUS ecosystem, a barcode is not just a string of numbers—it is a smart token, as real and transferable as currency or property rights. Through tokenization, CODEUS elevates the humble barcode into an asset class—one that is trackable, programmable, and interoperable across decentralized networks.

This transformation enables CODEUS AccelPass to turn every ticket into a smart wallet, or transform a bottle into a product with verified origin, limited edition status, and resale value. It's not merely a technical upgrade—it's a paradigm shift in how we conceptualize objects, data, and digital ownership.

—

Chapter 5:

Barcodes as Keys to the Blockchain

In the legacy retail ecosystem, barcodes function as simple identifiers—static symbols that point to records inside centralized databases. Their role is limited to encoding numeric data for product lookup, logistics, or pricing.

Within the CODEUS architecture, barcodes undergo a radical transformation: they become **keys to the blockchain**—unlocking real-time access to verifiable data, programmable rights, and decentralized ownership.

This repositions the barcode not as a passive tag, but as a dynamic access point. Once tokenized, a barcode gains the ability to interact with smart contracts, verify identity, trigger automated actions, and reference immutable on-chain metadata. It becomes, in essence, a physical or visual cryptographic key—a bridge between the physical world and the decentralized digital layer.

The Core Concept

Consider how a tokenized barcode functions:

- Each barcode links to a unique token (typically an NFT or similar asset) stored on a blockchain

- Scanning that barcode triggers a lookup—not in a traditional product database, but in a decentralized ledger

- What's retrieved isn't just a SKU or price, but could include:

  - Proof of ownership

  - Authenticity verification

  - Access credentials

  - Smart contract execution logic

  - Metadata such as expiration, history, or embedded media

The barcode acts as a key to on-chain truth. The scan isn't just reading a label; it's querying a blockchain.

Why This Matters

Traditional barcodes point to information that can be tampered with, duplicated, or mismanaged. Blockchain-based systems are immutable, trustless, and globally accessible. When barcodes become tokenized:

- Ownership can be verified without intermediaries

- Access rights (like event entry or product redemption) can be granted or revoked programmatically

- Metadata is no longer siloed—it's transparent, permissionless, and current

- Authenticity can be proven cryptographically, not merely asserted

This is especially powerful in environments where fraud prevention, access control, and trust are paramount—such as ticketing, luxury goods, pharmaceuticals, and identity verification.

How It Works in Practice

Here's a typical CODEUS AccelPass flow:

1. A barcode is generated and minted as a token on the blockchain

2. The token includes metadata like event details, validity period, issuer and original owner, and rights (fast-pass access, collectible media, loyalty perks)

3. The barcode (a visual alias of the token ID or contract address) is embedded on a ticket or product

4. When scanned, the CODEUS system queries the blockchain using the encoded reference, retrieves the token's current status, and determines what access or rights the holder has—optionally triggering a smart contract

This is not just a scan—it's a real-time handshake with a decentralized ledger.

Use Cases

Application	What the Barcode Unlocks
Event Ticketing	Access, fast-pass privileges, AR content, collectibles
Product Authenticity	Verifies originality, tracks ownership history
Supply Chain Transparency	Reveals sourcing, custody, and compliance
Loyalty & Rewards	Triggers token accrual based on purchases
Redemption Systems	Unlocks digital goods, discounts, or physical prizes

Every use case treats the barcode not as a static ID but as a programmable access point to a blockchain-anchored record.

The Strategic Advantage

By enabling every barcode to function as a blockchain key, CODEUS unlocks capabilities that traditional infrastructure cannot match:

- Interoperability across platforms (Amazon, Shopify, event platforms)

- Built-in rights management

- Secondary markets and resale support

- Real-time analytics powered by decentralized state checks

- Automated royalty or loyalty logic encoded on-chain

This approach turns physical objects and printed codes into gateways to programmable digital value—an Internet of Barcodes, where every code is both a unique asset and a trusted verifier.

Part III:

CODEUS Applications

Chapter 6:

CODEUS Global Code

The CODEUS Global Code represents the fundamental building block of the CODEUS ecosystem—a tokenized barcode that exists simultaneously in the physical and digital realms.

What is a CODEUS Global Code?

A CODEUS Global Code is a standard UPC or EAN barcode that has been minted as a blockchain token. This process transforms a simple numeric identifier into a smart, verifiable digital asset with embedded logic and metadata.

Each Global Code maintains backward compatibility with existing retail systems while adding layers of functionality:

- **Legacy Support**: Scans normally in traditional retail systems

- **Blockchain Layer**: When scanned with CODEUS-enabled systems, reveals full token data

- **Smart Contract Integration**: Can execute programmed logic upon scan

- **Ownership Trail**: Complete provenance from manufacture to current holder

- **Metadata Rich**: Product specifications, certifications, warranty information stored on-chain

Creating a Global Code

The process of creating a CODEUS Global Code:

1. A valid UPC/EAN number is assigned to a product

2. The barcode is minted as a token on the blockchain

3. Product metadata is attached to the token

4. Smart contract logic is programmed (optional)

5. The physical barcode is printed on the product

6. Token ownership is assigned to the manufacturer/brand

Applications Across Industries

Consumer Products: Verify authenticity, track ownership transfers, enable peer-to-peer resale with automated royalties

Electronics: Link serial numbers to blockchain records, activate warranties upon first scan, track repair history

Fashion & Luxury Goods: Combat counterfeiting, provide certificates of authenticity, enable authenticated resale markets

Food & Beverage: Track farm-to-table journey, verify organic/fair trade certifications, enable recall precision

Pharmaceuticals: Ensure supply chain integrity, prevent counterfeit medications, track cold chain compliance

Part IV:

CODEUS AccelPass

Chapter 7:

CODEUS AccelPass for Events

CODEUS AccelPass transforms every ticket into a smart wallet that lives on the blockchain. More than just digital admission, AccelPass utilizes tokenized barcode technology to create comprehensive, interactive experiences designed to unlock new revenue streams, deepen fan engagement, and deliver high-impact brand sponsorships—all while maintaining a frictionless, secure experience for attendees, organizers, merchants, and sponsors.

Vision: A Night to Remember

You've just purchased your ticket to see your favorite artist live. This isn't just any ticket—this is a CODEUS AccelPass Smart Ticket.

Arrival: A Wallet That Greets You

As soon as your purchase confirms, a secure AccelPass Smart Wallet is created for you on the blockchain containing your digital ticket, preloaded loyalty points, a curated welcome video from the artist, and AR filters for the venue.

Entry: Tap & Go

You arrive at the venue and tap your phone. The gate scans your blockchain-verified AccelPass—entry is instant. Onscreen displays your access tier, unlocked benefits like meet & greet access, and available perks like a free beverage. A staff member greets you by name and hands you a wristband with embedded AR capabilities.

Inside: Gamified, Personalized, Alive

As you explore, you receive real-time notifications rewarding engagement—loyalty points for visiting the merch tent, rare NFT collectibles for photo opportunities, behind-the-scenes content accessible via CODEUS Smartcode scans. Each moment is saved to your AccelPass timeline—a personal vault of your experience.

Interactions: Queue-Free Everything

Your AccelPass acts as a FastPass—tap to order food and grab when ready, skip lines. Scan to purchase merchandise and receive both physical products and blockchain-certified digital twins ready for your online avatar.

The Show: You're Part of It

During the performance, you participate in real-time song voting for the encore. AR effects sync with the music, customized to your preferences. The artist recognizes top fans—your engagement earned that moment.

After the Show: The Night Lives On

The next morning, your AccelPass updates with a personalized highlight reel blending official footage and your captures, an NFT badge of attendance, exclusive discounts to the next tour, and loyalty upgrade based on your engagement.

Your AccelPass Smart Wallet now carries memories, perks, and proof of your place in music history.

Sporting Events Application

The same technology transforms sporting events:

Purchase triggers AccelPass activation with team tokens and exclusive NFT welcome packs. VIP parking is automatically activated upon arrival. Entry is seamless with one tap.

In-stadium experiences include real-time trivia challenges, fan voting on predictions, exclusive audio feeds, and AR challenges. Merchandise purchases include blockchain-certified digital twins. Post-game updates include highlight reels featuring you, NFT badges of attendance with final scores, invitations to exclusive events, and verified superfan status carrying weight for future access and team governance participation.

Business Model Innovation

CODEUS AccelPass creates multiple revenue streams:

- **Dynamic Pricing**: Smart contracts enable real-time ticket pricing based on demand

- **Resale Royalties**: Artists and venues receive percentage of secondary market sales

- **Sponsorship Integration**: Brands pay for featured placement in fan wallets

- **Gamification Revenue**: In-event purchases driven by loyalty point systems

- **Data Monetization**: Aggregated, anonymized engagement data valuable to sponsors

- **Digital Collectibles**: NFTs create new merchandise categories

- **Access Tiers**: Programmable VIP experiences with automated upgrades

Chapter 8:

CODEUS SecurePass

In an era of globalized commerce, counterfeiting, supply chain opacity, and data fraud remain critical threats to brands, distributors, and consumers. CODEUS SecurePass addresses these issues by transforming simple barcodes into powerful tools for authentication and transparency.

What is CODEUS SecurePass?

CODEUS SecurePass is a blockchain-based system that converts any standard barcode into a Smartcode—a secure, data-rich digital asset. Rather than simply representing a SKU or inventory ID, each Smartcode acts as a verifiable, immutable token carrying complete ownership and history records, anchored on public or private blockchain.

Every scan enables stakeholders to instantly verify who originally manufactured the product, who owns it currently, whether it's genuine or tampered with, where it's been in the supply chain, and whether it has passed compliance checkpoints.

Vision: Trust at Every Scan

You're considering purchasing a luxury skincare serum. The brand uses CODEUS SecurePass.

At the Store: Scan for Truth

You pick up the product and scan the barcode. Your phone opens a CODEUS Smart Portal showing product authentication, manufacturing location and batch number, verified distribution chain, and tamper-evident history. You even see the timestamp of when the barcode was minted on the blockchain. This barcode tells a verifiable story.

After Purchase: Ownership Transfer

The moment you buy, your scan triggers ownership transfer on the blockchain. Your wallet holds a digital certificate of ownership, purchase timestamp, unique product DNA (batch plus serial hash), and options to leave reviews or receive direct recall notifications.

Going Deeper: The Origin Trail

Viewing the product journey reveals a visual map: verified GMP-certified manufacturing facility, documented shipping via verified freight companies, cold-chain logistics with temperature logs, laboratory testing results, and retail partner verification. Every checkpoint has a cryptographic stamp—immutable, transparent.

Resale or Recycling: A New Life

When you later sell the unused product on a secondary marketplace, CODEUS SecurePass enables digital ownership transfer. The new buyer sees the full provenance. Trust is restored in peer-to-peer resale. Or you recycle and your scan rewards you with eco-points, verified by blockchain as part of the brand's sustainability program.

Supply Chain Manager Perspective

As a supply chain manager for an electronics brand, CODEUS SecurePass provides unprecedented visibility:

Manufacturing: The Origin Point

As products are boxed, each is tagged with a CODEUS SecurePass Smartcode—blockchain-linked and minted with QA reports, assembly completion logs, and geo-location tags. The factory dashboard updates in real-time with all units authorized for transit.

Packaging & QA: Verified Before Movement

Workers scan each product before shipment. Automated QA reports and tamper-proof seals are logged. SecurePass creates digital certificates of readiness. Any manipulation after this point will be flagged.

Shipping: Blockchain Meets Logistics

As products load into CODEUS-integrated carriers, container barcodes are scanned and linked to inventory. GPS tracking embeds into each stage. Cold chain requirements log temperature and humidity. Checkpoints update automatically throughout the journey. Route deviation or condition anomalies trigger instant notifications.

Warehousing: Real-Time Inventory Intelligence

Upon arrival, receiving dock scans of SecurePass Smartcodes instantly confirm authenticity, batch integrity, chain of custody, and auto-sync with ERP and blockchain

—

records. CODEUS flags suspicious units where seal data doesn't match factory records for quarantine.

Retail Distribution: Traceable to the Shelf

Retail partners access read-only blockchain history showing complete product journey, verified authenticity, and tamper-evident audit trails. Consumers scanning at shelf see authentication confirmation and complete travel history.

Returns, Recalls, or Recycling: Instant Resolution

When recalls are necessary, CODEUS SecurePass locates affected units in seconds, verifies exact ownership trails, and triggers smart recall via blockchain with zero ambiguity. No guesswork, no liability exposure—just controlled, data-backed action.

The Problem It Solves

- **Counterfeit Products**: Fake products cause billions in losses and erode consumer trust. SecurePass provides tamper-proof ownership trails

- **Gray Market Diversion**: Products meant for specific regions or channels often appear elsewhere. SecurePass verifies route integrity and authorized resale

- **Data Fragmentation**: Supply chain records are often siloed across manufacturers, 3PLs, and retailers. SecurePass brings unified, on-chain visibility

- **Regulatory Compliance**: In sectors like pharmaceuticals or electronics, proving chain-of-custody is critical. SecurePass logs each handoff with cryptographic proof

Key Features

- Immutable ownership logs

- Tamper-evident tracking

- Real-time visibility across stakeholders

- API integrations for ERP, WMS, and POS systems

- Public or consortium blockchain compatibility

- Decentralized authentication (no single point of failure)

Industry Applications

Pharmaceuticals: Ensure drug authenticity and secure regulatory reporting

Electronics: Authenticate devices, track resale, verify warranties

Luxury Goods: Prove provenance and combat counterfeits

Apparel: Track product lineage from manufacturing to boutique

Automotive Parts: Verify OEM sourcing and recall integrity

Part V:

The Transformation

Chapter 9:

From GS1 to CODEUS

Understanding the evolution from traditional barcode systems to blockchain-based tokenization requires examining the current infrastructure and its limitations.

The GS1 System

GS1 is the private company that has managed the global barcoding system since the early 1970s (originally as the Uniform Code Council).

Owned and operated by major retail chains including Walmart, Kroger, Home Depot, and Lowe's, GS1 maintains the master database of UPC barcode numbers.

The GS1 model deserves credit for creating a unified global system. By ensuring all barcodes originated from a single database, they established uniqueness and prevented chaos in inventory management.

However, the GS1 system has significant limitations:

Centralization: Single point of control and potential failure

Cost Barriers: Expensive initial fees and annual renewals prohibit many small businesses

Static Data: Barcodes point to external databases with no intrinsic verification

No Ownership Transfer: Once assigned, barcodes cannot easily change hands or track secondary markets

Limited Functionality: Barcodes can only identify products, not authenticate them, track their journey, or enable programmable logic

CODEUS as Evolution, Not Replacement

CODEUS does not seek to replace the GS1 numbering system. Valid UPC numbers remain essential for retail compatibility. Instead, CODEUS adds a transformative layer on top of existing infrastructure.

A CODEUS-tokenized barcode:

- Maintains its valid GS1-originated UPC number

- Functions normally in traditional retail scanning systems

- Simultaneously exists as a blockchain token with extended capabilities

- Enables verification, ownership transfer, and programmable logic

- Provides supply chain transparency while respecting existing retail relationships

This approach ensures backward compatibility while unlocking future potential.

The Alternative Ecosystem

Beyond GS1, companies like Buyabarcode.com and TheBarcodeRegistry.com provide legitimate alternatives by reselling barcodes originally purchased from GS1 before annual fee structures were implemented. These services make barcodes more accessible to small businesses while maintaining validity.

CODEUS builds on this accessibility by offering tokenization services that work with any legitimate UPC source—whether from GS1 directly or from alternative providers—democratizing access to blockchain-enhanced barcode technology.

Chapter 10:

Implementation and Integration

Adopting CODEUS technology requires understanding the practical steps for integration into existing business operations.

For Product Manufacturers

Step 1: Barcode Acquisition

Obtain valid UPC numbers through GS1, Buyabarcode.com, or TheBarcodeRegistry.com. Ensure you have proper documentation (original GS1 certificate and letter of affiliation) for retail acceptance, particularly for Amazon and Walmart.

Step 2: CODEUS Tokenization

Submit barcode numbers to CODEUS platform for blockchain minting. Define metadata to be attached to tokens (product specifications, certifications, warranty terms). Program smart contract logic if desired (expiration, transfer rules, redemption conditions). Receive confirmation of token creation and blockchain address.

Step 3: Integration

Implement CODEUS SDK into existing systems or use CODEUS API for custom integration. Configure scanning infrastructure to recognize tokenized barcodes. Train staff on new capabilities and customer-facing benefits.

Step 4: Physical Implementation

Print barcodes on products as usual—they remain backward compatible. Optionally add CODEUS branding or QR code linking to blockchain verification portal. Update packaging or marketing materials to highlight tokenization benefits.

For Retailers and Distributors

Recognition: Existing scanning infrastructure works normally with CODEUS-tokenized barcodes

Enhancement: Optional integration with CODEUS verification systems provides authenticity checking

Benefits: Reduced counterfeit exposure, improved supply chain visibility, enhanced customer trust

——

Data Access: Real-time blockchain queries provide product history beyond traditional databases

For Event Organizers

AccelPass Integration: Connect existing ticketing systems to CODEUS AccelPass API. Define access tiers, loyalty point structures, and gamification elements. Configure venue scanning infrastructure for blockchain verification.

Fan Engagement: Design AR experiences, digital collectibles, and interactive elements. Create sponsor integration opportunities within fan wallets. Establish secondary market rules and royalty structures.

For Consumers

Access: Download CODEUS mobile app or use web-based scanning portal

Verification: Scan product barcodes to view blockchain-verified information

Ownership: Automatically receive ownership tokens upon purchase

Engagement: Participate in loyalty programs, access exclusive content, verify authenticity

Technical Architecture

Blockchain Layer: Ethereum-compatible smart contracts for token standards (ERC-721 for NFTs, ERC-1155 for hybrid), public or consortium blockchain options, gas optimization for cost-effective minting

Data Layer: IPFS/Arweave for decentralized media storage, on-chain metadata for critical information, encrypted private data for sensitive supply chain details

Application Layer: RESTful APIs for system integration, mobile SDKs for iOS and Android, web portals for verification and management, webhook notifications for real-time updates.

Security Considerations

Private key management for token control, multi-signature wallets for organizational accounts, encryption for sensitive data, audit trails for all token operations, compliance with data protection regulations.

Conclusion:

The Barcode Reimagined

For over fifty years, the barcode has served as one of commerce's most fundamental technologies. Its simplicity and universality made it indispensable. Yet throughout its history, the barcode remained fundamentally limited—a passive identifier pointing to external data, vulnerable to fraud, incapable of verification, and unable to evolve with the digital age.

CODEUS represents the natural evolution of barcode technology for the blockchain era. By tokenizing barcodes, we transform them from simple identifiers into programmable digital assets with intrinsic value, verifiable authenticity, and embedded intelligence.

The Transformation Summary

Traditional barcodes tell you WHAT something is. CODEUS barcodes tell you what something is, where it's been, who owns it, whether it's authentic, and what it can do.

This transformation unlocks unprecedented possibilities:

- Consumers gain confidence through verifiable authenticity and transparent supply chains

- Brands establish direct relationships with customers that persist beyond point of sale

- Retailers reduce fraud and improve inventory intelligence

- Event organizers create immersive experiences that drive engagement and revenue

- Supply chains achieve transparency that was previously impossible

- Secondary markets operate with trust and automated royalty distribution

- Smart contracts enable automation that reduces costs and friction

The Path Forward

The blockchain revolution is not coming—it's here. Tokenization is transforming assets across industries. CODEUS brings this transformation to the most ubiquitous commercial technology in existence.

As blockchain infrastructure matures and adoption accelerates, tokenized barcodes will become the standard, not the exception. Early adopters will establish competitive advantages in authenticity, customer engagement, and operational efficiency.

The question is not whether barcodes will be tokenized, but when your barcodes will be tokenized.

A New Paradigm

CODEUS doesn't just add features to barcodes—it fundamentally reconceives what a barcode can be. From passive label to active asset. From simple identifier to cryptographic key. From isolated data point to node in a global trust network.

The future of barcodes is not about better printing or more digits. It's about transformation from physical to digital, from centralized to decentralized, from static to programmable.

That future is CODEUS.

The barcode has been reimagined. The technology is ready. The infrastructure is being built.

Welcome to the future of barcodes.

—

Bonus Material:

Navigating the Current Barcode Landscape

Bonus A:

The GS1 System – A Brief History

Understanding CODEUS's place in the barcode ecosystem requires understanding the system it builds upon. GS1 represents both the foundation and the limitation of traditional barcode infrastructure.

Origins of the Global Standard

The barcode itself predates GS1 by decades. Norman Joseph Woodland and Bernard Silver invented the first barcode in 1951, though practical implementation required waiting for scanning technology to catch up.

In the late 1960s, telecom giant GTE developed computer scanners capable of reading barcodes, but a critical problem remained: every retailer operated their own isolated barcode system.

The chaos was unsustainable. Each retailer assigned its own barcodes, meaning manufacturers needed different codes for different stores. There was no universal database, no standardization, no interoperability.

The Uniform Code Council (UCC), now known as GS1, emerged in the early 1970s to solve this problem. Their solution was elegantly simple: create a centrally managed database of barcode numbers. If all UPC barcodes originated from the same source, uniqueness could be guaranteed globally.

The strategy worked. GS1 convinced retailers worldwide to adopt this unified system, creating the infrastructure that enabled modern commerce. This achievement deserves recognition—they built a system that transformed retail operations and enabled global supply chain coordination.

The Current Structure

GS1 is not a governmental organization. It is a private consortium owned and operated by major retail chains including Walmart, Kroger, Home Depot, and Lowe's. This ownership structure creates both stability and tension—the system is funded by those who benefit most from it, but also controlled by entities with significant commercial interests.

Over time, GS1's pricing model has become increasingly prohibitive for small businesses. Initial fees and annual renewals (ranging from $150 to $3,500+ annually) present significant barriers to entry. For entrepreneurs who have invested most of their capital in product development, these fees can be deal-breakers.

Historical Context: The First Barcode

The first UPC barcode successfully used in commerce was scanned on June 26, 1974, at a Marsh Supermarket in Troy, Ohio. The product: a pack of Wrigley's Juicy Fruit chewing gum. That pack of gum now resides in the Smithsonian Institution, a symbol of how a simple technology transformed global commerce.

Bonus B:

The Alternative Ecosystem

Beyond the Monopoly

While GS1 maintains the master database, they are not the only source for obtaining valid UPC numbers. Alternative providers emerged when GS1's pricing model became prohibitive for small businesses.

The key principle: barcodes must originate from GS1 to ensure uniqueness, but they need not be purchased directly from GS1. Companies that acquired large blocks of barcodes from GS1 before the implementation of annual fees in 2002 can legally resell those numbers without passing annual costs to customers.

The Legitimate Alternative: Buyabarcode.com

Buyabarcode.com, founded in 1999, pioneered this model. By purchasing barcodes from GS1 before annual fee structures were implemented, they could offer:

- Single barcode purchases (not just fixed quantities of 1, 10, 100, etc.)

- No annual renewal fees

- Immediate delivery with proper documentation

- Access to GS1 US Data Hub for major retailer compliance

The company has been featured in The Wall Street Journal and The Washington Post as a viable GS1 alternative, and served as a consultant to Amazon during their early barcode verification implementation.

Other legitimate alternatives include TheBarcodeRegistry.com, which operates on a similar model.

The Critical Distinction: Valid vs. Fraudulent

The success of legitimate alternatives spawned fraudulent imitators. These "wildcat" sellers create barcodes through two methods:

1. Fabricating numbers without GS1 validation

2. Hijacking dormant GS1 prefixes without authorization

These fraudulent barcodes fail at major retailers, particularly Amazon and Walmart, forcing businesses to reprint expensive packaging after discovering their codes don't work.

Bonus C:

Verification Framework
The Five Essential Questions

Before purchasing barcodes from any source, businesses should demand answers to five critical questions:

1. Do your barcodes originate from GS1?

This establishes the fundamental legitimacy of the numbering. Without GS1 origin, the barcodes are not globally unique and will fail at major retailers.

2. Can you provide a copy of the original GS1 certificate after purchase?

Legitimate sellers can instantly provide documentation showing their prefix was officially issued by GS1. This certificate includes the company name, prefix number, and issuance date.

3. Can you provide a signed Letter of Affiliation?

This document establishes the legal connection between the seller and the GS1 certificate holder. It authorizes the transfer of barcode usage rights and is essential for major retailer acceptance.

4. Do you have access to the GS1 US Data Hub?

The GS1 US Data Hub is GS1's proprietary database required by Walmart, Kroger, and other major retailers. Without Data Hub access, products cannot be listed at these retailers regardless of barcode validity.

5. Will you place my company, barcodes, and products into the GS1 US Data Hub?

This is the final validation step. Legitimate sellers with Data Hub access will register your products, enabling immediate acceptance at major retailers.

The Bright Line Test

If a seller cannot answer "YES" to all five questions, they are not a legitimate barcode provider. No exceptions. The consequences of using invalid barcodes include:

- Rejection by Amazon, Walmart, and major retailers

- Costly packaging reprints

- Delayed product launches

- Potential conflicts with other businesses using the same numbers

Bonus D:

Platform-Specific Requirements

Amazon's Verification Process

Amazon's barcode fraud problem reached crisis proportions as the marketplace grew. Their solution: mandatory verification for all new product listings.

When listing a product, Amazon cross-references your UPC with the GS1 GEPIR database. If your company name doesn't match the prefix owner exactly, you'll receive this error:

"ERROR: You are using UPC, EAN, ISBN, ASIN, or GTIN codes that do not match the products you are trying to list. If you believe you have reached this message in error, please contact Seller Support."

Resolution requires opening a support ticket and uploading two documents:

1. Original GS1 certificate for your barcode prefix

2. Signed Letter of Affiliation from the certificate holder

Once verified, your prefix is "whitelisted" for all future listings. This one-time verification applies to all products using the same prefix.

Important Clarifications:

- Existing listings are grandfathered— current products won't be removed

- Verification is per-prefix, not per-product

- Support tickets typically resolve within 24-48 hours

- Amazon support: (866) 216-1072

Walmart's Data Hub Requirement

Walmart, as a GS1 co-owner, enforces the strictest barcode requirements. All products must exist in the GS1 US Data Hub before Walmart will accept them for listing.

This creates only two pathways for Walmart sellers:

1. Purchase barcodes directly from GS1 (with annual fees)

2. Purchase from a Data Hub-enabled reseller (Buyabarcode.com or TheBarcodeRegistry.com)

There are no workarounds. Products without Data Hub registration cannot be sold at Walmart, regardless of barcode validity elsewhere.

Bonus E:

CODEUS Integration with Current Systems

Backward Compatibility

CODEUS tokenization doesn't replace traditional barcodes—it enhances them.

A CODEUS-tokenized barcode:

- Retains its original GS1-issued number

- Scans normally in legacy retail systems

- Meets Amazon and Walmart verification requirements

- Simultaneously exists as a blockchain token with extended capabilities

This dual existence ensures businesses can adopt CODEUS technology without disrupting existing retail relationships or requiring infrastructure changes from retail partners.

Migration Path

Businesses with existing GS1 or legitimate alternative barcodes can tokenize them through CODEUS platforms. The process:

1. Verify barcode legitimacy (must meet the five-question test)

2. Submit for blockchain minting with desired metadata

3. Receive token confirmation and blockchain address

4. Print barcodes as usual—they remain backward compatible

5. Optionally add CODEUS verification QR codes or branding

The Bridge to Tomorrow

Understanding the current barcode landscape—its history, its limitations, its gatekeepers, and its legitimate alternatives—provides essential context for understanding CODEUS's transformative potential.

GS1 built the foundation. Alternative providers made it accessible. CODEUS makes it intelligent, verifiable, and programmable.

The future doesn't abandon the past—it builds upon it.

Bonus F:

Resources

Legitimate Barcode Sources:

- GS1: www.gs1us.org

- Buyabarcode.com: www.buyabarcode.com

- TheBarcodeRegistry.com: www.thebarcoderegistry.com

Verification Resources:

- GS1 GEPIR Database: www.gepir.gs1.org

- GS1 US Data Hub: (accessible through active GS1 accounts)

Platform Support:

- Amazon Seller Support: (866) 216-1072

- Walmart Seller Support: seller.walmart.com/support

CODEUS Resources:

- CODEUS Platform: [contact information]

- Technical Documentation: [documentation link]

- Developer API: [API documentation link]

About the Author

For more than 25 years, Erik Quisling has been known in the business world as "The Barcode Guru".

In the earlier days of Amazon he worked as a strategic barcode consultant helping to unravel some of their most daunting barcode challenges.

As the founder of online barcode giants Buyabarcode.com and TheBarcodeRegistry.com, Erik has literally helped thousands of companies successfully launch millions of products onto store shelves around the world. With his new company, CODEUSai.com, Erik has become the world's leading thought leader and innovator for the future of barcodes.

For more information, please visit us at:

https://www.CODEUSai.com

www.ingramcontent.com/pod-product-compliance
Lightning Source LLC
Chambersburg PA
CBHW060633210326
41520CB00010B/1580